The North Ship

THE
NORTH
SHIP

by

PHILIP LARKIN

FABER AND FABER

London · Boston

First published in 1945
First published in cased edition 1966
First published in this edition 1973
by Faber and Faber Limited
3 Queen Square London WC1
Reprinted 1975, 1977 and 1979
Printed in Great Britain by
Whitstable Litho Ltd., Whitstable, Kent
All rights reserved

ISBN 0 571 10503 3 (Faber Paperbacks)

To
S.L. and E.E.L.
in gratitude

CONDITIONS OF SALE

© 1966 by Philip Larkin

Contents

Introduction

THE NORTH SHIP would probably not have been published if the late William Bell, then an undergraduate at Merton College, had not set about making up a collection which he eventually called *Poetry From Oxford in Wartime*. Oxford poetry was reputedly in the ascendant again following the scarlet and yellow *Eight Oxford Poets* in 1941 (Keith Douglas, Sidney Keyes, John Heath-Stubbs, Drummond Allison, *et al.*), and Bell no doubt thought it was time for another round-up. When his anthology came out in 1944 it had Allison, Heath-Stubbs and Roy Porter from the earlier collection, and the new names of Bell himself, Francis King, myself, Christopher Middleton and David Wright. How many of the second group had been in hard covers before I don't know: certainly I hadn't.

Before it appeared, however, the proprietor of the small but then well-known house that was producing the book wrote to some of its contributors enquiring if they would care to submit collections of their own work. The letter I received was on good-quality paper and signed with an illegible broad-nibbed squiggle: I was enormously flattered, and typed out some thirty pieces on my father's old portable Underwood. The publisher seemed to like them, saying that he could undertake publication early next year 'and perhaps have the book ready in February'. Since this was already the end of November, my excitement ran high, but I must (with memories of *The Writers' and Artists' Year Book*) have parried with some enquiry about terms, for another letter a month later (two days before Christmas) assured me that no agreement was necessary.

Looking at the collection today, it seems amazing that anyone should have offered to publish it without a cheque in advance and a certain amount of bullying. This, however, was not how I saw it at the time. As February turned to March, and March to April, my anticipation of the promised six copies curdled through exasperation to fury and finally to indifference; my astonishment to find now, on looking up the records, that in fact they arrived almost exactly nine months after despatch of typescript (on 31st July 1945) shows how completely I subsequently came to believe my own fantasy of eighteen months or even two years. I inspected them sulkily.

It may not have been the best introduction to publication: my Oxford friend, Bruce Montgomery, was writing Edmund Crispin novels for Gollancz, while Routledge had taken up Keyes and Heath-Stubbs. Still, I was on the same list as Dylan Thomas, Roy Fuller, Nicholas Moore and other luminaries, and the book was nicely enough produced, with hardly any misprints; above all, it was indubitably *there*, an ambition tangibly satisfied. Yet was it? Then, as now, I could never contemplate it without a twinge, faint or powerful, of shame compounded with disappointment. Some of this was caused by the contents but not all: I felt in some ways cheated. I can't exactly say how. It was a pity they had ever mentioned February.

ii

Looking back, I find in the poems not one abandoned self but several – the ex-schoolboy, for whom Auden was the only alternative to 'old-fashioned' poetry; the under-graduate, whose work a friend affably characterized as 'Dylan Thomas, but you've a sentimentality that's all your own'; and the immediately post-Oxford self, isolated in Shropshire with a complete Yeats stolen from the local girls' school. This search for a style was merely one aspect of a general immaturity. It might be pleaded that the war years were a bad time to start writing poetry, but in fact the principal poets of the day – Eliot, Auden, Dylan Thomas, Betjeman – were all speaking out loud and clear, and there was no reason to become entangled in the undergrowth of *Poetry Quarterly* and *Poetry London* except by a failure of judgment. Nor were my contemporaries similarly afflicted. I remember looking through an issue of *The Cherwell*, one day in Blackwell's, and coming across John Heath-Stubbs's 'Leporello': I was profoundly bewildered. I had never heard of Leporello, and what sort of poetry was this – who was he copying? And his friend Sidney Keyes was no more comforting: he could talk to history as some people talk to porters, and the mention of names like Schiller and Rilke and Gilles de Retz made me wish I were reading something more demanding than English Language and Literature. He had most remarkable brown and piercing eyes: I met him one day in Turl Street, when there was snow on the ground, and he was wearing a Russian-style fur hat. He stopped, so I suppose we must have known each other to talk to – that is, if we had had anything to say. As far as I remember, we hadn't.

The predominance of Yeats in this volume deserves some explanation. In 1943 the English Club was visited by Vernon Watkins, then stationed at an Air Force camp nearby; impassioned and imperative, he swamped us with Yeats until, despite the fact that he had not nearly come to the end of his typescript, the chairman had forcibly to apply the closure. As a final gesture Vernon distributed the volumes he had been quoting from among those of us who were nearest to him, and disappeared, exalted, into the black-out. I had been tremendously impressed by the evening and in the following weeks made it my business to collect his books up again – many of them were limited Cuala Press editions, and later Yeats was scarce at that time – and take them to him at Bradwell, where he was staying with some people called Blackburn who kept a goat. This time Vernon read me Lorca.

As a result I spent the next three years trying to write like Yeats, not because I liked his personality or understood his ideas but out of infatuation with his music (to use the word I think Vernon used). In fairness to myself it must be admitted that it is a particularly potent music, pervasive as garlic, and has ruined many a better talent. Others found it boring. I remember Bruce Montgomery snapping, as I droned for the third or fourth time that evening *When such as I cast off remorse, So great a sweetness flows into the breast . . .*, 'It's not his job to cast off remorse, but to earn forgiveness.' But then

Bruce had known Charles Williams. Every night after supper before opening my large dark green manuscript book I used to limber up by turning the pages of the 1933 plum-coloured Macmillan edition, which stopped at 'Words for Music Perhaps', and which meant in fact that I never absorbed the harsher last poems. This may be discernible in what I wrote.

When reaction came, it was undramatic, complete and permanent. In early 1946 I had some new digs in which the bedroom faced east, so that the sun woke me inconveniently early. I used to read. One book I had at my bedside was the little blue *Chosen Poems of Thomas Hardy*: Hardy I knew as a novelist, but as regards his verse I shared Lytton Strachey's verdict that 'the gloom is not even relieved by a little elegance of diction'. This opinion did not last long; if I were asked to date its disappearance, I should guess it was the morning I first read 'Thoughts of Phena At News of Her Death'. Many years later, Vernon surprised me by saying that Dylan Thomas had admired Hardy above all poets of this century. 'He thought Yeats was the greatest by miles', he said. 'But Hardy was his favourite.'

iii

'F/Sgt. Watkins, V' was the book's kindest and almost only critic. Writing from the Sergeants' Mess, he was generously encouraging (did I recall his Yeats anecdote: 'Always I encourage, always'?), reserving for only one or two pieces his sharpest term of condemnation, 'not a final statement'. 'Yesterday', he added, 'I destroyed about two thousand poems that mean nothing to me now.' Despite this hint, although with considerable hesitation, the book is now re-published, as there seems to be still some demand for it. I have corrected two misprints and one solecism. As a coda I have added a poem, written a year or so later, which, though not noticeably better than the rest, shows the Celtic fever abated and the patient sleeping soundly.

P. L.

October 1965.

I

(To Bruce Montgomery)

All catches alight
At the spread of spring:
Birds crazed with flight
Branches that fling
Leaves up to the light—
Every one thing,
Shape, colour and voice,
Cries out, Rejoice!
      A drum taps: a wintry drum.

Gull, grass and girl
In air, earth and bed
Join the long whirl
Of all the resurrected,
Gather up and hurl
Far out beyond the dead
What life they can control—
All runs back to the whole.
      A drum taps: a wintry drum.

What beasts now hesitate
Clothed in cloudless air,
In whom desire stands straight?
What ploughman halts his pair
To kick a broken plate
Or coin turned up by the share?
What lovers worry much
That a ghost bids them touch?
      A drum taps: a wintry drum.

Let the wheel spin out,
Till all created things
With shout and answering shout
Cast off rememberings;

Let it all come about
Till centuries of springs
And all their buried men
Stand on the earth again.
    A drum taps: a wintry drum.

II

This was your place of birth, this daytime palace,
This miracle of glass, whose every hall
The light as music fills, and on your face
Shines petal-soft; sunbeams are prodigal
To show you pausing at a picture's edge
To puzzle out the name, or with a hand
Resting a second on a random page—

The clouds cast moving shadows on the land.

Are you prepared for what the night will bring?
The stranger who will never show his face,
But asks admittance; will you greet your doom
As final; set him loaves and wine; knowing
The game is finished when he plays his ace,
And overturn the table and go into the next room?

III

The moon is full tonight
And hurts the eyes,
It is so definite and bright.
What if it has drawn up
All quietness and certitude of worth
Wherewith to fill its cup,
Or mint a second moon, a paradise?—
For they are gone from earth.

Dawn

To wake, and hear a cock
Out of the distance crying,
To pull the curtains back
And see the clouds flying—
How strange it is
For the heart to be loveless, and as cold as these.

Conscript
(for James Ballard Sutton)

The ego's county he inherited
From those who tended it like farmers; had
All knowledge that the study merited,
The requisite contempt of good and bad;

But one Spring day his land was violated;
A bunch of horsemen curtly asked his name,
Their leader in a different dialect stated
A war was on for which he was to blame,

And he must help them. The assent he gave
Was founded on desire for self-effacement
In order not to lose his birthright; brave,
For nothing would be easier than replacement,

Which would not give him time to follow further
The details of his own defeat and murder.

VI

Kick up the fire, and let the flames break loose
To drive the shadows back;
Prolong the talk on this or that excuse,
Till the night comes to rest
While some high bell is beating two o'clock.
Yet when the guest
Has stepped into the windy street, and gone,
Who can confront
The instantaneous grief of being alone?
Or watch the sad increase
Across the mind of this prolific plant,
Dumb idleness?

VII

The horns of the morning
Are blowing, are shining,
The meadows are bright
  With the coldest dew;
The dawn reassembles.
Like the clash of gold cymbals
The sky spreads its vans out
  The sun hangs in view.

Here, where no love is,
All that was hopeless
And kept me from sleeping
  Is frail and unsure;
For never so brilliant,
Neither so silent
Nor so unearthly, has
  Earth grown before.

Winter

In the field, two horses,
Two swans on the river,
While a wind blows over
A waste of thistles
Crowded like men;
And now again
My thoughts are children
With uneasy faces
That awake and rise
Beneath running skies
From buried places.

For the line of a swan
Diagonal on water
Is the cold of winter,
And each horse like a passion
Long since defeated
Lowers its head,
And oh, they invade
My cloaked-up mind
Till memory unlooses
Its brooch of faces—
Streams far behind.

Then the whole heath whistles
In the leaping wind,
And shrivelled men stand
Crowding like thistles
To one fruitless place;
Yet still the miracles
Exhume in each face
Strong silken seed,

That to the static
Gold winter sun throws back
Endless and cloudless pride.

Climbing the hill within the deafening wind
The blood unfurled itself, was proudly borne
High over meadows where white horses stood;
Up the steep woods it echoed like a horn
Till at the summit under shining trees
It cried: Submission is the only good;
Let me become an instrument sharply stringed
For all things to strike music as they please.

How to recall such music, when the street
Darkens? Among the rain and stone places
I find only an ancient sadness falling,
Only hurrying and troubled faces,
The walking of girls' vulnerable feet,
The heart in its own endless silence kneeling.

X

Within the dream you said:
Let us kiss then,
In this room, in this bed,
But when all's done
We must not meet again.

Hearing this last word,
There was no lambing-night,
No gale-driven bird
Nor frost-encircled root
As cold as my heart.

Night-Music

At one the wind rose,
And with it the noise
Of the black poplars.

Long since had the living
By a thin twine
Been led into their dreams
Where lanterns shine
Under a still veil
Of falling streams;
Long since had the dead
Become untroubled
In the light soil.
There were no mouths
To drink of the wind,
Nor any eyes
To sharpen on the stars'
Wide heaven-holding,
Only the sound
Long sibilant-muscled trees
Were lifting up, the black poplars.

And in their blazing solitude
The stars sang in their sockets through the night:
'Blow bright, blow bright
The coal of this unquickened world.'

XII

Like the train's beat
Swift language flutters the lips
Of the Polish airgirl in the corner seat.
The swinging and narrowing sun
Lights her eyelashes, shapes
Her sharp vivacity of bone.
Hair, wild and controlled, runs back:
And gestures like these English oaks
Flash past the windows of her foreign talk.

The train runs on through wilderness
Of cities. Still the hammered miles
Diversify behind her face.
And all humanity of interest
Before her angled beauty falls,
As whorling notes are pressed
In a bird's throat, issuing meaningless
Through written skies; a voice
Watering a stony place.

XIII

I put my mouth
Close to running water:
Flow north, flow south,
It will not matter,
It is not love you will find.

I told the wind:
It took away my words:
It is not love you will find,
Only the bright-tongued birds,
Only a moon with no home.

It is not love you will find:
You have no limbs
Crying for stillness, you have no mind
Trembling with seraphim,
You have no death to come.

Nursery Tale

All ı remember is
The horseman, the moonlit hedges,
The hoofbeats shut suddenly in the yard,
The hand finding the door unbarred:
And I recall the room where he was brought,
Hung black and candlelit; a sort
Of meal laid out in mockery; for though
His place was set, there was no more
Than one unpolished pewter dish, that bore
The battered carcase of a carrion crow.

So every journey that I make
Leads me, as in the story he was led,
To some new ambush, to some fresh mistake:
So every journey I begin foretells
A weariness of daybreak, spread
With carrion kisses, carrion farewells.

The Dancer

Butterfly
Or falling leaf,
Which ought I to imitate
In my dancing?

And if she were to admit
The world weaved by her feet
Is leafless, is incomplete?
And if she abandoned it,
Broke the pivoted dance,
Set loose the audience?
Then would the moon go raving,
The moon, the anchorless
Moon go swerving
Down at the earth for a catastrophic kiss.

The bottle is drunk out by one;
At two, the book is shut;
At three, the lovers lie apart,
Love and its commerce done;
And now the luminous watch-hands
Show after four o'clock,
Time of night when straying winds
Trouble the dark.

And I am sick for want of sleep;
So sick, that I can half-believe
The soundless river pouring from the cave
Is neither strong, nor deep;
Only an image fancied in conceit.
I lie and wait for morning, and the birds,
The first steps going down the unswept street,
Voices of girls with scarves around their heads.

XVII

To write one song, I said,
As sad as the sad wind
That walks around my bed,
Having one simple fall
As a candle-flame swells, and is thinned,
As a curtain stirs by the wall
—For this I must visit the dead,
Headstone and wet cross,
Paths where the mourners tread,
A solitary bird,
These call up the shade of loss,
Shape word to word.

That stones would shine like gold
Above each sodden grave,
This, I had not foretold,
Nor the birds' clamour, nor
The image morning gave
Of more and ever more,
As some vast seven-piled wave,
Mane-flinging, manifold,
Streams at an endless shore.

XVIII

If grief could burn out
Like a sunken coal,
The heart would rest quiet,
The unrent soul
Be still as a veil;
But I have watched all night

The fire grow silent,
The grey ash soft:
And I stir the stubborn flint
The flames have left,
And grief stirs, and the deft
Heart lies impotent.

Ugly Sister

I will climb thirty steps to my room,
Lie on my bed;
Let the music, the violin, cornet and drum
Drowse from my head.

Since I was not bewitched in adolescence
And brought to love,
I will attend to the trees and their gracious silence,
To winds that move.

XX

I see a girl dragged by the wrists
Across a dazzling field of snow,
And there is nothing in me that resists.
Once it would not be so;
Once I should choke with powerless jealousies;
But now I seem devoid of subtlety,
As simple as the things I see,
Being no more, no less, than two weak eyes.

There is snow everywhere,
Snow in one blinding light.
Even snow smudged in her hair
As she laughs and struggles, and pretends to fight;
And still I have no regret;
Nothing so wild, nothing so glad as she
Rears up in me,
And would not, though I watched an hour yet.

So I walk on. Perhaps what I desired
—That long and sickly hope, someday to be
As she is—gave a flicker and expired;
For the first time I'm content to see
What poor mortar and bricks
I have to build with, knowing that I can
Never in seventy years be more a man
Than now—a sack of meal upon two sticks.

So I walk on. And yet the first brick's laid.
Else how should two old ragged men
Clearing the drifts with shovels and a spade
Bring up my mind to fever-pitch again?
How should they sweep the girl clean from my heart,
With no more done
Than to stand coughing in the sun,
Then stoop and shovel snow onto a cart?

The beauty dries my throat.
Now they express.
All that's content to wear a worn-out coat,
All actions done in patient hopelessness,
All that ignores the silences of death,
Thinking no further than the hand can hold,
All that grows old,
Yet works on uselessly with shortened breath.

Damn all explanatory rhymes!
To be that girl!—but that's impossible;
For me the task's to learn the many times
When I must stoop, and throw a shovelful:
I must repeat until I live the fact
That everything's remade
With shovel and spade;
That each dull day and each despairing act

Builds up the crags from which the spirit leaps
—The beast most innocent
That is so fabulous it never sleeps;
If I can keep against all argument
Such image of a snow-white unicorn,
Then as I pray it may for sanctuary
Descend at last to me,
And put into my hand its golden horn.

XXI

I dreamed of an out-thrust arm of land
Where gulls blew over a wave
That fell along miles of sand;
And the wind climbed up the caves
To tear at a dark-faced garden
Whose black flowers were dead,
And broke round a house we slept in,
A drawn blind and a bed.

I was sleeping, and you woke me
To walk on the chilled shore
Of a night with no memory,
Till your voice forsook my ear
Till your two hands withdrew
And I was empty of tears,
On the edge of a bricked and streeted sea
And a cold hill of stars.

One man walking a deserted platform;
Dawn coming, and rain
Driving across a darkening autumn;
One man restlessly waiting a train
While round the streets the wind runs wild,
Beating each shuttered house, that seems
Folded full of the dark silk of dreams,
A shell of sleep cradling a wife or child.

Who can this ambition trace,
To be each dawn perpetually journeying?
To trick this hour when lovers re-embrace
With the unguessed-at heart riding
The winds as gulls do? What lips said
Starset and cockcrow call the dispossessed
On to the next desert, lest
Love sink a grave round the still-sleeping head?

XXIII

If hands could free you, heart,
   Where would you fly?
Far, beyond every part
Of earth this running sky
Makes desolate? Would you cross
City and hill and sea,
   If hands could set you free?

I would not lift the latch;
   For I could run
Through fields, pit-valleys, catch
All beauty under the sun—
Still end in loss:
I should find no bent arm, no bed
   To rest my head.

Love, we must part now: do not let it be
Calamitous and bitter. In the past
There has been too much moonlight and self-pity:
Let us have done with it: for now at last
Never has sun more boldly paced the sky,
Never were hearts more eager to be free,
To kick down worlds, lash forests; you and I
No longer hold them; we are husks, that see
The grain going forward to a different use.

There is regret. Always, there is regret.
But it is better that our lives unloose,
As two tall ships, wind-mastered, wet with light,
Break from an estuary with their courses set,
And waving part, and waving drop from sight.

Morning has spread again
Through every street,
And we are strange again;
For should we meet
How can I tell you that
Last night you came
Unbidden, in a dream?
And how forget
That we had worn down love good-humouredly,
Talking in fits and starts
As friends, as they will be
Who have let passion die within their hearts.
Now, watching the red east expand,
I wonder love can have already set
In dreams, when we've not met
More times than I can number on one hand.

XXVII

Heaviest of flowers, the head
Forever hangs above a stormless bed;
Hands that the heart can govern
Shall be at last by darker hands unwoven;
Every exultant sense
Unstrung to silence—
The sun drift away.

And all the memories that best
Run back beyond this season of unrest
Shall lie upon the earth
That gave them birth.
Like fallen apples, they will lose
Their sweetness at the bruise,
And then decay.

XXVIII

Is it for now or for always,
The world hangs on a stalk?
Is it a trick or a trysting-place,
The woods we have found to walk?

Is it a mirage or miracle,
Your lips that lift at mine:
And the suns like a juggler's juggling-balls,
Are they a sham or a sign?

Shine out, my sudden angel,
Break fear with breast and brow,
I take you now and for always,
For always is always now.

XXIX

Pour away that youth
That overflows the heart
Into hair and mouth;
Take the grave's part,
Tell the bone's truth.

Throw away that youth
That jewel in the head
That bronze in the breath;
Walk with the dead
For fear of death.

XXX

So through that unripe day you bore your head,
And the day was plucked and tasted bitter,
As if still cold among the leaves. Instead,
It was your severed image that grew sweeter,
That floated, wing-stiff, focused in the sun
Along uncertainty and gales of shame
Blown out before I slept. Now you are one
I dare not think alive: only a name
That chimes occasionally, as a belief
Long since embedded in the static past.

Summer broke and drained. Now we are safe.
The days lose confidence, and can be faced
Indoors. This is your last, meticulous hour,
Cut, gummed; pastime of a provincial winter.

The North Ship
Legend

I saw three ships go sailing by,
Over the sea, the lifting sea,
And the wind rose in the morning sky,
And one was rigged for a long journey.

The first ship turned towards the west,
Over the sea, the running sea,
And by the wind was all possessed
And carried to a rich country.

The second turned towards the east,
Over the sea, the quaking sea,
And the wind hunted it like a beast
To anchor in captivity.

The third ship drove towards the north,
Over the sea, the darkening sea,
But no breath of wind came forth,
And the decks shone frostily.

The northern sky rose high and black
Over the proud unfruitful sea,
East and west the ships came back
Happily or unhappily:

But the third went wide and far
Into an unforgiving sea
Under a fire-spilling star,
And it was rigged for a long journey.

65° N.

My sleep is made cold
By a recurrent dream
Where all things seem
Sickeningly to poise
On emptiness, on stars
Drifting under the world.

When waves fling loudly
And fall at the stern,
I am wakened each dawn
Increasingly to fear
Sail-stiffening air,
The birdless sea.

Light strikes from the ice:
Like one who near death
Savours the serene breath,
I grow afraid,
Now the bargain is made,
That dream draws close.

70° N.

Fortunetelling.

"You will go a long journey,
In a strange bed take rest,
And a dark girl will kiss you
As softly as the breast
Of an evening bird comes down
Covering its own nest.

"She will cover your mouth
Lest memory exclaim
At her bending face,
Knowing it is the same
As one who long since died
Under a different name."

75° N.

Blizzard

Suddenly clouds of snow
Begin assaulting the air,
As falling, as tangled
As a girl's thick hair.

Some see a flock of swans,
Some a fleet of ships
Or a spread winding-sheet,
But the snow touches my lips

And beyond all doubt I know
A girl is standing there
Who will take no lovers
Till she winds me in her hair.

Above 80° N.

"A woman has ten claws,"
Sang the drunken boatswain;
Farther than Betelgeuse,
More brilliant than Orion
Or the planets Venus and Mars,
The star flames on the ocean;
"A woman has ten claws,"
Sang the drunken boatswain.

Waiting for breakfast, while she brushed her hair,
I looked down at the empty hotel yard
Once meant for coaches. Cobblestones were wet,
But sent no light back to the loaded sky,
Sunk as it was with mist down to the roofs.
Drainpipes and fire-escape climbed up
Past rooms still burning their electric light:
I thought: Featureless morning, featureless night.

Misjudgment: for the stones slept, and the mist
Wandered absolvingly past all it touched,
Yet hung like a stayed breath; the lights burnt on,
Pin-points of undisturbed excitement; beyond the glass
The colourless vial of day painlessly spilled
My world back after a year, my lost lost world
Like a cropping deer strayed near my path again,
Bewaring the mind's least clutch. Turning, I kissed her,
Easily for sheer joy tipping the balance to love.

But, tender visiting,
Fallow as a deer or an unforced field,
How would you have me? Towards your grace
My promises meet and lock and race like rivers,
But only when you choose. Are you jealous of her?
Will you refuse to come till I have sent
Her terribly away, importantly live
Part invalid, part baby, and part saint?